Things that Suck

Things that Suck

Jason Kaplan

**Andrews McMeel
Publishing, LLC**

Kansas City • Sydney • London

10 11 12 13 14 RR2 10 9 8 7 6 5 4 3 2 1

ISBN-13: 978-0-7407-9760-6
ISBN-10: 0-7407-9760-3

Library of Congress Control Number: 2010921950

www.andrewsmcmeel.com

Attention: Schools and Businesses
Andrews McMeel books are available at quantity discounts with
bulk purchase for educational, business, or sales promotional use.
For information, please write to: Special Sales Department,
Andrews McMeel Publishing, LLC, 1130 Walnut Street,
Kansas City, Missouri 64106.

for mom and dad

two people with a positive outlook

I once felt sorry for myself because I had no shoes—until I met a man who had no feet.

Jewish proverb

I personally think we developed language because of our deep inner need to complain.

from Jane Wagner's *The Search for Signs of Intelligent Life in the Universe*

Are you like me?

Do you tend to complain a lot? Or do you just happen to find there are so many things to complain about. Maybe you experience schadenfreude* (let's hope not). Or maybe your spirit is lifted by thoughts of all the things that could go wrong, but don't.

Whatever the reason, I've compiled this list to make you feel better, not worse. Think of it as company for your misery, or a way to understand the world we've created and the variety of ways in which it screws us, each and every day. Think of it when you happen to be thinking, "Well, at least things couldn't get any worse."

If only that were true . . .

J.K.

*deriving pleasure from another's misfortune

Things that Suck:

getting fired

getting dumped

getting dumped right after buying someone a present

getting dumped on your birthday

traveling a long distance to see someone,
who then dumps you

getting dumped and fired on the same day

male pattern baldness

dandruff

censorship

book banning

gang violence

having your car stereo stolen

having your car window smashed

eating bad fish

food poisoning

chronic halitosis

putting your dog to sleep

bouncing a check

parking tickets

ulcers

leaky roofs

screaming babies

student loan payments

scraping the Teflon in your pan and getting
flaky black crud in your food

long supermarket lines

long supermarket lines when you're only buying one thing

getting your ATM receipt and seeing your account balance

getting burned in the kitchen

getting burned anywhere else

the smell of hair burning

the smell of tires burning

deforestation

fraternity hazing

neo-Nazis

racists, bigots, and assholes

your boss, probably

getting stuck next to someone with BO

having BO

having painful gas

running out of gas

homelessness

homework

flunking an exam

knowing you're going to flunk, five minutes in

sitting through the last 40 minutes of a class, waiting to turn in an exam that you've basically already flunked

erasing too hard and ripping the page

sneezing without a tissue and having to walk to the bathroom with your hand to your face

13

nuclear waste

politicians who mispronounce "nuclear"

not having what it takes

not waiting long enough to drip and having to walk around with a wet spot by your zipper

leaning against wet paint

splitting your pants

carpet stains

acid rain

acid reflux

acid-washed jeans

getting divorced

having parents who're getting divorced

getting shitty parents

low self-esteem

lactose intolerance

farting in church

farting in yoga

smelling someone else's fart

being at the gym, on a cardio machine, and deeply inhaling your neighbor's fart

meth labs

fender benders

pet dander

hay fever

people who won't shut up during movies

people who answer their phone during movies

people who text message during movies

finding a bug in your food
finding rat droppings under your toaster
bottom of your grocery bag dropping out
getting turned down for a loan
cavities
foot odor
bee stings
presidential election years
campaign promises
daytime talk shows
changing diapers
losing the pacifier
losing your luggage
ruining a surprise
getting poked in the eye
getting mugged
breaking a nail
breaking a heel
other things that involve stuff breaking
outbreaks
epidemics
pandemics
staying at the Bellevue-Stratford Hotel
in Philadelphia during the 1976
American Legion convention
diarrhea
vomiting
seeing someone else vomit
having diarrhea and vomiting simultaneously

dropping your ice cream in the dirt

needing a stronger eyeglass prescription

missing the first five minutes of a movie

pimples

cellulite

varicose veins

shampoo in your eye

wiping your ass with paper towels

toilet overflows

toilet won't flush

toilet won't flush at someone else's house

toilet overflows at someone else's house and
leaks out under the bathroom door

getting picked last for teams

getting splashed from the curb

getting taken in three-card Monte

losing a contact lens

dropping a lightbulb

finding out your ex is getting remarried

finding out at 3 A.M. the waiter gave you
regular instead of decaf

finding a horse's head under your covers

finding out you've had food in your
teeth . . . after your date

finding out you're dating the kind of person
who wouldn't tell you

poison ivy and poison oak

phone solicitors

bloody noses

missing your bus

going back to work after vacation

losing your address book

forgetting your keys

stepping in gum

stepping in dog shit

stepping in dog shit and tracking it inside

The Family Circus

blue laws

white flight

infomercials

headaches

migraines

dropping your wedding ring down the drain

dropping one thing behind another that's

really big and hard to move

drafty windows

late fees

litter

arthritis

splinters

hammering your thumb

getting shit on by a bird

getting stood up

getting sued

getting your fingers stuck together

with Krazy Glue

getting your finger stuck to your

eyelid with Krazy Glue

popping your bike chain
having your bike stolen
having your seat stolen
anal warts
genital warts
genital warts on someone else
other varieties of warts
name-droppers
star fuckers
horn honkers
holes in your socks
losing a sock
leaving a red sock in your white laundry
accidentally swigging from the beer bottle that
everyone's been ashing cigarettes into
obstructed views
out of delivery range
getting cut off in traffic
getting cut off when
you're trying to talk
getting cut
getting stuck in the
middle seat on an airplane
airplane seats
flying coach
flying the red-eye
airplane food
not getting fed on an airplane
double-edged swords

paying for water
sunburns
razor burns
ingrown hairs
dropping your cell phone
dropping your cell phone the day you buy it
dropped cell phone calls
going over your minute plan
talking to someone for several minutes before
realizing you've been disconnected
Internet dating
writer's block

turning 40

middle age

midlife crises

hemorrhoids

hemorrhagic fever

slamming your finger in a car door

walking through a spider's web

getting scratched by a cat

forgetting your password

forgetting your lunch

finding your newspaper in a puddle

the second and third *Matrix* movies

Jar Jar Binks

evil stepmothers

stock market crashes

frivolous lawsuits

ambulance chasers

dead batteries

missing your exit

missing your kids

identity theft

factory closings

bankruptcy

losing a parking spot

losing the White House

being put on hold

hold music

Kenny G

phone trees

foldout beds

detention

demerits

roaches

termites

terrorists

mothers-in-law

bitchy brides

being a bridesmaid for the eighth time

bridesmaid dresses

shopping for shoes to match

your ugly bridesmaid dress

the word "fiancé"

the room service in this place

burning the roof of your mouth

spam (Internet variety)

spam (canned variety)

junk mail

phone bills

electric bills

cable bills

stepping in a puddle

computer crashes

losing all your data

losing your wallet

losing a bet

losing a ticket

losing your nerve

losing your homecoming football game

global warming

lobbyists

allergies

smog

funerals

blackouts

dust in your eye

getting bumped from your flight

missing your connecting flight

umbrella flipping inside out

can't get the printer to work

can't see those Magic Eye pictures

ATM ate your card

dog ate your birthday cake

cat ate your fish

paper jams

hangnails

bad tippers

mimes

fruitcake

drum solos

used car salesmen

chipping your nail polish

falling off the wagon

running out of toilet paper

walking out of the bathroom with
toilet paper stuck to your shoe

walking down an airplane aisle with a toilet seat
cover hanging from the back of your pants

running out of hot water with shampoo in your hair

department store mirrors

trying on jeans

being told to calm down

credit card companies

the Taliban

April 15th

commercials with people singing about food

pumping diesel into your car instead of regular

driving away from the gas pump with the hose
still jammed in your tank

paying $1,300 to have a gas pump repaired

shopping for presents the day before Christmas

taking down your Christmas decorations

not taking down your Christmas decorations

**showing up at 4 A.M. to work Black
Friday at Walmart only to be
trampled to death by stampeding
bargain hunters**

fake butter

fake creamer

fake boobs

fake pecs

fake orgasms

wet dog smell

that hospital smell

**the smell of your teeth being
drilled at the dentist**

oh yeah, the dentist

the morning commute
the evening commute
the nightly news
the daily grind
overly perky people
people who think they're
great at British accents
striking out
the embargo against Cuba
pledge week on public radio
paying five dollars for coffee
coffee breath
drunk drivers
being grounded
breaking a mirror
parallel parking
potholes
dog bites
toxic waste
oil spills
WMDs
the Middle East peace conflict
the general lack of peace everywhere
security walls
drive-by shootings
school shootings
deadbeat dads
child support payments

dieting

trans fats

sugar-free candy

counting calories

hearing skinny people complain about

how fat they are

getting squirted in the eye with lemon

pen leaks in your pocket

pen leaks in your purse

pen breaks in your mouth

sitting on your glasses

leaving your cell phone in a cab

losing your cell phone

hurricanes

marzipan

the KKK

race riots

racial profiling

turbulence

wind shear

backseat drivers

car sickness

motion sickness

morning sickness

illegal dumping

insider trading

margin calls

bear markets

the deficit

plagiarism

libel

slander

gas prices

asbestos

asthma

Olestra

anal seepage

the runs

the squirts

the flu

high cholesterol

low blood sugar

diaper rash

urinary tract infections

**people who don't wash their
hands in the bathroom**

people who don't teach their kids to
wash their hands

Hummers

slumlords

militant vegans

overpackaging

getting your tongue stuck to a frozen pole

getting in trouble for something
you didn't do

**getting your eye shot out by a Red Ryder
carbine-action two-hundred-shot
range model air rifle**

rock hitting your windshield

forgetting your combination

back-ne

cankles

pit stains

backwash

wet willies

chapped lips

stretch marks

salad bar Jell-O

cold toilet seats

people who won't shut up

people who are way too into reggae

Americans at playing soccer

Europeans at watching soccer

your cell phone company

my cell phone company

cable going out

being out of shape

being homesick

sleeping with a snorer

people who slowly unwrap

candy in the theater

people who talk really, really
loudly on their cell phones

people who talk on their cell phones while
they're driving and don't pay attention

people who text message while driving and stay
parked at green lights

holes in your pockets
pebbles in your shoes
booster shots
accidentally letting go of your balloon
forcing bears to ride bicycles
pretending to have a conversation with your
friend's two-year-old on the phone
getting your braces tightened
losing your retainer
hunting for your kid's retainer in the garbage
noisy toys given by people without kids
noise pollution
electrocution
bird flu
ticks
and tics
hairballs
dust bunnies
dust mites
ear mites
learning to drive stick and
getting stuck on an incline
in front of a long line of traffic
being the passenger of a crappy driver
people who drive on the shoulder
people who drive 40 miles per hour in the passing lane
people who cut in at the last minute
**having your penis cut off by your wife and
tossed from a moving car window**

clogged arteries

clogged drains

speed traps

carjackers

gum disease

Mondays

bunions

blisters

corns

monsoons

earthquakes

landslides

radon leaks

smelly hippies

patchouli

Hacky Sackers

knots in your hair

knots in your shoelaces

creepy dudes

having your
credit card stolen

forgetting your credit card

at a restaurant

being rejected for a
new credit card

high interest payments

flunking your driver's exam

shopping in the "husky department"

being called "husky"

falling down stairs

pushed in the pool

wetting the bed

fumbling the ball

throwing an interception

failing remedial English

forced to repeat the fifth grade

**being the biggest kid in your class because
you were held back**

crashing your dad's car

graduating to an older demographic

not living up to your potential

regretting your lost youth

hangovers

hot flashes

menopause

charley horses

hucksters

hickeys

rehab

withdrawal

getting towed

getting booted

impound lots

house fires

speed bumps

land mines

coal dust explosions

being a coal miner

overcooked calamari

undercooked chicken

chicken pox

party poopers

carpetbaggers

going on strike

picketing

scabs

getting felt up in the subway

falling asleep in public and drooling on yourself

itchy wool

SATs

STDs

HMOs

stubbing your toe

hitting your funny bone

being puked on

constipation

the first day of school

mean teachers

sucking at math

being a poor speller

dyslexia

flat tires

wedgies

atomic wedgies

waiting for the school bus

waiting for the school bus in the rain

going to school where all the kids are dicks

purse snatchers

sweatshops

nasal spray addiction

getting short-changed

getting stuck behind a bus

polling the audience, phoning a friend, and
STILL getting the answer wrong

**starting your awesome road trip by
heading 200 miles in the wrong direction**

dropping your only quarter into
a grate below the parking meter

**figuring you'll only be gone five minutes,
and coming back to a $65 ticket**

ripping up the ticket in anger and getting
another one 60 days later for double the fine

**hearing about the doubled fine from your
father whose car it was**

hearing from your
father after his OTHER
car got towed on
your account

**paying for both the
doubled fine and getting your
father's car out of impound**

comparing this amount ($530) to
the amount it could have cost (25¢)

**hearing this story recounted
for everyone's amusement each Thanksgiving
for 18 years**

birds flying into windows

underwear skids

losing your health insurance

being on welfare

being stared at

being evicted

rent increases

loud neighbors

bad water pressure

sixth-floor walk-ups

having to shower in your kitchen

**getting scalded in the shower when
the toilet flushes**

having to share a toilet with your neighbors

**having to wait for your neighbor to finish so
you can use the bathroom**

having to wait for two
neighbors to finish
so you can use the
bathroom

et cetera

listening to your gross
neighbor having sex

**listening to your gross neighbor having sex
when you're not**

thin walls

lead paint

black mold

hearing a mouse eating your food

getting a great idea when you're high, then realizing
how stupid it was when you're not

running out of pot

running out of beer

running out of money for pot and/or beer

spilling bong water on your carpet

bad pot

bad acid

bad trips

flashbacks

short-term memory loss

wardrobe malfunctions

slippery floors

cigarette burns

nicotine stains

Dutch elm disease

drug cartels

overfishing

"ethnic cleansing"

paparazzi

**forgetting your
PIN number**

customer service

Live Strong bracelets

the woman in front of you at the market with
the huge stack of expired coupons

your refrigerator that won't stop buzzing

the kid kicking the back of your seat

that kid's parents

your golf game
your social life
your sex life
your career
your yearbook photo
your driver's license photo
"shock and awe"
heartburn
thorns
jock itch
getting to the Super Bowl four times and
never winning
getting shut out at the World Series
getting your dick caught in your zipper
getting gum stuck in your hair
getting gum out of your kid's hair
being made a scapegoat
being falsely accused of a crime
**being falsely
accused and
having to
run for your life**
searching for a one-armed
man who murdered your wife,
only no one believes you
having one arm
having no arms
OK, having no arms and no legs

mistakenly congratulating someone on being
pregnant when they're just overweight
having a crush on your best friend's girl
being allergic to your girlfriend's cat
barfing up sixty dollars' worth of sushi
blind dates
bad skin
delirium tremens
Big Tobacco
the Patriot Act
comb-overs
clear-cutting
clubbing baby seals
the first ding on your new car
getting caught lip-synching on live TV
lip-synching
lip service
insomnia
narcolepsy
incontinence
ingrown toenails
impertinent sales clerks
impertinent customers
tsunamis
tidal waves
swimming in paperwork
working late
working on the weekend
not getting paid overtime

undertows

overbookings

"past due" notifications

passing a kidney stone

overprescription of antidepressants for kids

overhearing someone talking trash about you

peeing on the side of the toilet

panty lines

bikini spiders

basement floods

redeployment

unemployment

your boyfriend's band

having to carry shit for your boyfriend's band

waiting up until 1 A.M. so you can carry it back

realizing, while camping, that you hate camping

being mauled by a bear

being attacked by a shark

kidnapping

dognapping

crow's feet

going gray

split ends

burnt toast

burnt coffee

bad art

rained-out games

paying for parking

parachute pants

living in a ghetto
living in Darfur
living a lie
living in an attic hoping the Nazis don't
find you, only they do
living stacked up in a tank of water with
rubber bands over your claws and
eventually getting boiled alive
living too close to an airport
living beside train tracks
living under a subway
living in a subway
pissing your pants
crapping your pants
blood in your stool
ants in your kitchen
ants at a picnic
hitting a dog with your car
hitting a deer with
your car
driving over a cat
having your pet
carried off by coyotes
getting fleeced

Ticketmaster
assassination
waterboarding
mercury in our fish
hormones in our food

infertility

sexual frustration

blue balls

bed bugs

art banning

propaganda

velvet ropes

being at the end of the line

throwing out your back

color blindness

river blindness

River Phoenix's untimely death

John Candy's untimely death

Phil Hartman's untimely death

dying young

struck by lightning

hit by hail

melanoma

carcinoma

**other things that
end in "noma"**

the DMV

slavery

child labor

child abuse

spousal abuse

sexual abuse

sexual misconduct

sexual harassment

runs in your stockings

going up a dress size

going up a pant size

going up for parole and getting turned down

going for broke and then actually going broke

going to a movie and finding it sold out

forgetting your lines

stage fright

panic attacks

heart attacks

dial-up

losing your baseball down the sewer

getting your Frisbee stuck on the roof

missing a spot with your sunscreen

running out of propane in the
middle of a barbecue

**running out of booze in the
middle of a party**

running out of time when you're
trying to defuse a bomb

gold diggers

skinflints

cheapskates

backstabbers

chickenshits

brownnosers

sycophants

malcontents

margarine

smoke detector beeping at 2 A.M.
because the battery is weak

oversleeping

waking up in the morning

waking up on the wrong side of the bed

waking up in a strange bed

**waking up in a strange bed with your arm
stuck beneath a strange person**

texting someone you're into,
then wondering if they got it because
you haven't heard back, even though you're
pretty sure they did

waiting forever for your subway train

drug pushers

arms dealers

warmongers

meter maids

cock teasers

philanderers

co-op boards

dealing with a committee

seeing a bird with a
six-pack ring stuck around its neck

dropping your toothbrush in the toilet

staining your favorite shirt

losing your lucky shirt

losing money on a hot stock tip

mom finding your porn

dad finding your bong

broken condoms

out of condoms

getting your high school girlfriend pregnant

getting your high school girlfriend pregnant,
except you're not in high school anymore

getting knocked up

being left at the altar

being told the end of a movie you haven't seen

triple bogeys

missing a four-inch putt

DVD skipping

TiVo not recording last 10 minutes of the game

can't afford TiVo

locking yourself out of your house

locking yourself out of your car

**locking yourself out of your car with
the engine still running**

dripping faucets

hard water

losing an earring

rejected from college

expelled from college

expelled from high school

milk money stolen by a bully

rental agency running out of cars

mom forgetting your birthday

husband forgetting your anniversary

unrequited love

unfulfilled dreams

71

corrupt judges
detached retinas
distended testicles
athlete's foot
pickpockets
brain freeze
brain drain
crotch rot
pink slips
pay cuts
nicotine addiction
bombing on stage
losing your inspiration
strip searches
strip mining
Streptococcus
small talk
talking to someone who spends the whole time looking around for someone else to talk to
hanging with someone who spends the whole time either texting or on the phone
cramps
carbuncles
crimes against humanity
Lincoln assassination
Kennedy assassination
Martin Luther King assassination
New Orleans' levies
being expendable

constantly being called Chinese
when you're actually Korean
being complimented on your English
even though you were born here
watching someone clip their nails on the subway
losing the remote control
learning the truth about Santa Claus
changing schools when you're a kid
being forced to eat your vegetables
flushing your goldfish
tripping and falling
tripping and falling in a public place
tripping while you're waiting tables and
spilling food all over your customer
being the customer
being arrested
being arrested and reported on in the news
getting shanked
getting the shit kicked out of you
getting frozen in carbonite
getting locked in the chokey
getting stiffed for a tip
stale ice
stale cake
skunky beer
bagels outside of New York
pizza outside of New York
commercials in the movies
chlorofluorocarbons

talking to a spitter

jaywalking tickets

getting your lawn TP'ed

getting your mailbox knocked over

having a cross burned outside your house

lynching

gay bashing

Vioxx

Fen-Phen

thalidomide

embolisms

aneurysms

mealy apples

mushy pickles

lumpy oatmeal

indigestion

hernias

getting caught rubbing one out

getting caught rubbing one out
to a picture of Katie Couric

dental dams

cock blocking

cane toads

caning

canned peas

canned laughter

ragweed

frostbite

liver spots

running into someone and forgetting their name
when you have to introduce them

**having your name forgotten by someone you know
and being forced to introduce yourself**

getting your girlfriend's name tattooed on your arm
then breaking up

**breaking up with someone and forgetting a cool
sweatshirt at their place**

dating someone with a giant tattoo of their ex's name
emblazoned across their chest

crystal meth

tartar

tax audits

dogfighting

cockfighting

horse doping

housing projects

bitten by a mosquito

stung by a hornet

stuck in a rut

misuse of the word "ironic"

Gulf War syndrome

the military-industrial complex

post-traumatic stress disorder

pork barrel spending

getting kicked in the nuts

getting punched in the boob

getting dumped

by text message

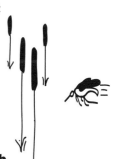

pop-up ads
"friendly" fire
carbon emissions
nocturnal emissions
Ikea on a weekend
walking through a screen door
walking into a glass door
running into a tree
running into someone you can't stand
running into your ex who dumped you
and they're on a date
the Man
Whitey
bitches what only wants my money
having to live on dried ramen noodles
the value of the dollar
traveling across an international border with
heroin-filled condoms in your stomach
failing the bar exam multiple times
the LSAT
the MCAT
the GRE
stalkers
flashers
shaving cuts
pink eye
scratching your shades
refugee camps
family feuds

having to travel with all of your liquids in a Ziploc
having to take off your shoes at the airport
having to take off your shoes in people's houses
can't find a sitter
can't carry a tune
can't remember the last
time you "got some"
losing your memory
losing your passion
losing your mind
losing count and having to start all over
people who love trying to make you
lose count by going, "twelve, nineteen,
eighty-four, two, eleven, forty-five . . ."
living downwind from a cattle farm
being cattle
cults
rats
narcs
squealers
tattletales
copycats
line butters
Peeping Toms
blister-paks
heat waves
bomb shelters
Ponzi schemes
Amway parties

tennis elbow

foot fungus

nosebleed seats

having the wrong leg operated on

worrying about money

waiting tables when you're an actor

waiting for the phone to ring

waiting for the governor to call

waiting for the axe to fall

tree falling on your house

chick falling out of its nest

dropping an egg

dropping the ball

losing a big account

dry cleaner losing your shirt

finding someone in your secret fishing spot

getting a fish hook caught in your face

casting back, hooking your buddy,
casting forward

pinched nerves

fourth place

shitty advice

testing positive

shipping and handling

legal mumbo jumbo

fine print

red tape

cold food that's supposed to be hot

hot food that's supposed to be cold

rusty pipes
brown water
infected wounds
bad scars
douche bags
death squads
fascism
dictators
totalitarianism
kangaroo courts
news broadcasts that find it appropriate
to play patriotic music in the background
rhetoric
partisan politics
out of paper
out of toner
out of memory
out of time
out of range
no signal
no vacancy
no more tables (at least not for you)
inflation
weeds
road rage
not knowing
that sinking feeling
that feeling of doom
Nam

housing foreclosures
the subprime mortgage crisis
real estate prices
learning disabilities
guys who talk at your tits
guys who wear too much cologne
guys who come up behind you in the office
and massage your shoulders
bird smugglers
ivory dealers
animal poachers
big game hunters
blood diamonds
blow-up beds
cold sores
getting a cold sore right before a date
herpes simplex
hepatitis
losing a hubcap
having a flat ass
working the nightshift
cleaning off graffiti
cleaning that black gunk that
builds up in your shower
breaking someone's heart
having your heart broken
having no one to kiss New Year's Eve
not being anyone's Valentine
realizing you've been an ass

not being believed when you're telling the truth
not being believed after being abducted by aliens
being probed
being insecure
insensitivity
missing by only one number
killing your houseplants
moldy fruit that you just bought two days ago
plastic fork breaks while eating carryout
barbecue rained out
social climbers
narcissists
that new guy in accounting
nuclear weapons
loose nukes
power surges
urethral catheters
impossible deadlines
missing the FedEx guy
prescription drug prices
lies
the rumor mill
double standards
false modesty
glass ceilings
getting stuck under a vent
freezing your ass off
stepping from a curb into ankle-deep slush
leaking out of your boobs during a fancy dinner

Monday-morning quarterbacks

armchair pundits

guests that don't know when to leave

Big Brother

big government

monopolies

planned obsolescence

living in a doorway

living out of your car

car stalling

waiting for a tow truck

looking at your food in a restaurant as it
waits under a heat lamp

phony people

people who act as if they like you
when you know they don't

**people who think the sun shines
out of their butt**

armrest hogs

alarm clocks

raw papaya

itchy ass

beached whales

stuff from RadioShack

most radio stations

packing for a trip

unpacking after a trip

getting carded when you're 18

not getting carded when you're 28

your roommate's dirty dishes

your roommate's annoying girlfriend

people who won't move into the intersection and make you miss the turn

steep driveways that make you scrape the bottom of your car

people who put "my benz" or "my bmr" on the license plates of their "Benz" or "Beemer"

having a really small penis

people who yell "Free Bird" in rock shows

white dudes who think they're black

having your New Year's party shut down at 10 minutes to midnight by the cops

getting a toenail disease after not wearing flip-flops for 10 minutes in a Russian bathhouse

spoiled brats

misbehaved kids

child beauty pageants

animal cruelty

supermarket sushi

supermarket tomatoes

droughts

dry spells

wildfires

hot flashes

dizzy spells

custody battles

idling trucks

exhaust fumes

root canals

red-eye

jury duty

blackmail

plumber's butt

the executives at Enron

pawning your stuff

asking your parents for money

hearing bad news

getting sneezed on

getting sneezed on by a dog

getting sneezed on by a camel

getting outed for using JDate

being put up for adoption

being returned to the orphanage

having to interview for kindergarten

being told to "talk to the hand"

buzzing a bald patch into your beard

discovering, after a land survey,
that part of your house sits on
someone else's property

your dot-com already registered

your brilliant idea already done

your favorite theater turned
into a drugstore

being too short to ride a roller coaster

having to wait an hour
after eating before you're
allowed to go swimming

blacklisted

blackballed

outbid

turned down

passed over

left out

burned out

bitched out

washed up

water weight

back fat

love handles

man boobs

going to the emergency room

rejected for health insurance

being uninsured

**having insurance that doesn't
cover anything**

car crashes

whiplash

state-run hospitals

bill collectors

bad karma

abortion

getting waxed

getting stuck with a bar tab

getting lost in a bad neighborhood

being stuck in a job you hate

using the same razor blade for six months

being too dumb

being a third wheel

being ditched

being sold a fake

being sold a ten-dollar bag of oregano

being used to make someone else jealous

being in love with someone who doesn't
give a crap about you

growing pains

teething

Montezuma's Revenge

great old building being torn down

favorite show getting cancelled

pubic hair in the soap

constantly having to reboot

constantly having to remind someone

constantly being reminded

constantly having to ask

constantly being told what to do

viruses

floods

pestilence

vermin

bad signage

poor drainage

prison

adult acne

shitty haircuts

scratched records

child molesters

home wreckers

fleas

Salmonella

Listeria

mad-cow disease

Internet addiction

privacy invasion

smoke in your hair

mowing the lawn

shoveling snow

scraping ice off your windshield

skiing into a pole

sledding into a tree

compound fractures

claustrophobia

xenophobia

acrophobia

et cetera

being lost

losing your passport

being stranded

needing adult diapers

bleeding cuticles

getting your car keyed

trouble catching a cab

rat dying behind your wall

putting on sunscreen

when you're hairy

writing a screenplay next to someone
who's also writing a screenplay
people's screenplays
not getting credit
not feeling appreciated
not finding out in time
being replaced
being obsolete
being overqualified
overdrawing your account
insufficient funds
surprised by your Visa bill
constantly being asked why
you aren't married
great dream interrupted
neighbor's dog won't stop barking
neighbor's toilet leaks
into your kitchen
neighbor's shower backs up
into your bathtub
moving to a faster line that
immediately becomes slower
than your old line
lending something and
not getting it back
borrowing something
and breaking it
lending something and getting
it back broken

stiff necks

head nods

beer goggles

bag worms

moth holes

pop quizzes

plastic grocery bags

high-fructose corn syrup

secondhand smoke

sloppy seconds

swallowing a bug

cleaning up dog barf

accidentally touching gum under a table

accidentally touching a dried

booger under a table

accidentally touching a not-so-dried

booger under a table

being at fault

getting ratted out

having to apologize

fighting with your best friend

spilling oil onto a hot

engine manifold and lighting

your car on fire

landfills

living near a landfill

lifting your suitcase and

pulling the handle off

lifting your hamster and pulling the tail off

losing a big fish
losing your will
losing your way
nightmares
cold sweats
paper cuts
pee stains
being laughed at
being inadequate
being switched at birth
being left for a younger woman
being left because someone suddenly
decided they were gay
being overruled
being guilt-tripped
being ignored
always coming second
Dear John letters
breaking up
"It's not you, it's me"
men
women
wild-goose chases
gutter balls
know-it-alls
whiners

wearing a costume to a party that—surprise—
is actually not a costume party
pretending to be interested

having to hide a boner in public

being unable to avoid taking the world's
longest shit while you're on a date

waiting for your date, who you hardly know,
to take the world's longest shit

trying to shit quietly when someone
you barely know is on the other side of the door

being too shy

being too tall

. . . too fat

. . . too short

. . . too hairy

. . . too old

being criticized

being a hypochondriac

dating a hypochondriac

being allergic to peanuts

being allergic to chocolate

dropping your air conditioner
out the window

listening to someone
you have a crush on
talk about someone else

being called the wrong
name during sex

sleeping in the wet spot

discovering someone
is not the person
you thought they were

last call

baby talk

mood swings

tiny backpacks

unsolicited advice

having a dumb name

having the same name as a celebrity

having a lazy eye

having a fatwa issued against you

having to get your nasal passages cauterized

having to get recircumcised

rain the day after you wash your car

sitting beside someone with loud headphones

piercing your eardrum

dropping your iPod

splitting your lip

biting your tongue

breaking your leg

being accident prone

walking on crutches

walking across ice on crutches

losing your receipt

getting store credit instead
of your money back

trying to open a milk carton but
the spout doesn't push forward
and you have to pick at it,
and it gets all shaggy and fucked up

breaking a promise
having a promise broken
having your stomach pumped
recovering from surgery
waiting for test results
waiting in the waiting room
waiting on hold for 45 minutes,
then getting disconnected
getting a "time-out"
getting cut from the team
getting banned from the building
getting $80 from the ATM, but
the receipt says you got $100
getting marketing texts
you have to pay for
getting call after call when
someone's fax machine keeps
auto-dialing the wrong number
taking off work to
wait for the cable guy,
but he never shows
alimony
stage moms
coffee jitters
not being able to
find a bathroom
discovering your fly's been
unzipped all day

discrimination

contaminated beaches

smelling someone's burp

dating an ass

taking a suave sip and spilling your drink

down your shirt

spilling coffee into your keyboard

spilling Diet Coke into your friend's computer

having to buy someone a new laptop

revolving debt

rush hour

traffic

pneumonia

double pneumonia

leaving the iron on

setting the toaster, walking away, and

coming back to realize it wasn't plugged in

flipping over your handlebars

betting on the wrong horse

discovering the dog
crapped in the house

climbing into bed and discovering

the dog peed on your mattress

racist dogs

racist parrots

ungrateful children

being written out of the will

pretending to be happy for
people who are jerks

crappy movie remakes

cronyism

nepotism

bureaucrats

rectal exams

venereal disease

panty crickets

staph infections

premature ejaculation

irritable bowel syndrome

carpal tunnel syndrome

people who say, "What can I do you for?"

deleting a message you wanted to keep

waking up your foot when it falls asleep

remembering you forgot something

forgetting something you
just remembered

craving something and then
regretting it after

eating disorders

skinny bitches

yappy dogs

fluorescent lighting

stressing out

speeding tickets

a certain L.A. traffic
cop whose initials are L.K.

finding a worm in your apple

finding half a worm in your apple

119

breaking a shoelace

cracking a tooth

Lee Harvey Oswald

John Wilkes Booth

ozone depletion

extinction

angina

hair in your food

sand in your vagina

head lice

rubella

postpartum depression

flavorless fruit

unlawful possession

skanky hotel rooms

telemarketing calls

mistakenly seeing

your grandfather's balls

bad hair days

the hiccups

being afraid

Nazi Youth rallies

Mercury in retrograde

pollution

apathy

shoddy construction

posers

rip-offs

erectile dysfunction

not finding your size
never finding your size
always wearing hand-me-downs
running out of ice
imitation bacon (a.k.a. fakon)
hearing about a party you weren't invited to
finding out someone's been cheating on you
people who cheat on other people
cheaters
haters
liars
tailgaters
SUVs
SUV drivers who park in compact spaces
forcing your dog to take medicine
rubbing ointment on
your cat's butthole
freaking out
obsessing
queefing
hat hair
mud slides
middle names
shrinking biodiversity
steroids in our food
steroids in our sports
tractor trailer jackknifes
crashing your motorcycle
wiping out on your bike

Agent Orange

yellow snow

being abandoned

being forced to go fishing

being blindsided

waiting for luggage

being antsy

amnesia

accidentally e-mailing your entire contact list
to your entire contact list

gagging

choking

swallowing a filling

getting a fishbone caught in your throat

burning the dinner you're about
to serve to ten guests who are
starting to arrive

collapsing your soufflé

trying to think

people who are
too loud in the library

wiping asses

being too young

. . . too bony

. . . too ordinary

. . . too different

. . . too something that's hard to pinpoint
but just feels wrong

slave labor

slave wages

spilt milk

stuttering

psychotic exes

sitting on a tack

exposing your filmrunning aground

barnacles

turncoats

traitors

rickets

catch-22s

sleeping in a box

sleeping in your own vomit

sleeping beside someone you're fighting with

waiting for a pot to boil

losing the lottery

paying for overtime

water poisoning

living below a noisy person

being hit with a water balloon

E. coli in the spinach

coffee pot overflows, getting
grounds in everything

eating something out of the fridge

that you thought was tasty

but later realize is six weeks old

ice that tastes like garlic

water that smells like fish

advice about how to raise your children
from people without kids

having your TiVo filled up by your kid's
Hannah Montana marathon

hearing your kid repeat something
inappropriate they heard you say in front of
the person you said it about

seeing your kid pick up something
off the street and eat it

farting a tiny package in your pants
and having to throw away your
underwear in a public restroom

spider veins

nipple hair

ear hair

needing bifocals

needing to clean out your fridge

squeezing out too much lotion

athletes who take steroids
then lie about it when
they're caught

people who don't take
no for an answer

people who love to hear
themselves talk

people who are always referring
to events as a sea change

. . . or a paradigm shift

. . . or a perfect storm

not challenging a word in Scrabble that
turns out not to be a word

having your seven-letter Scrabble word messed up

the cost of getting married

the cost of getting divorced

paying for your daughter to marry a guy who
she ends up divorcing eight months later

homicide

genocide

patricide

lots of stuff that ends in -cide

taking a fun little trip south of the border then
discovering you need your passport to get back

blowing your nose with paper towels

customers who steal your toilet paper

waiters who try to take your plate
before you're finished

unruly bush

accidentally peeing when
you sneeze

. . . or cough

. . . or laugh

college tuition payments

wearing a hot dress to a
party where not only is someone
else wearing the same thing
but looks better in it than you do

finding your first gray hair

finding your first gray pube

throwing up a small amount in your mouth

needing a toothpick for a really long time

taking a drunken piss while talking on your phone
and dropping it in the toilet

losing that little needle-thing you use
to inflate basketballs

the Macarena

your kid's friends

your kid's friends' parents

having all the food in your fridge go bad
during a blackout

having all the food in your restaurant go bad
during a blackout

showboats

smarty-pantses

butt-in-skies

blowhards

knuckleheads

jerks that don't hold the door

people who leave a carpet of
spit-out sunflower seed
shells behind them in the
movie theater

your upstairs neighbor's
two-year-old who's learning to run

old sponge smell

cheap plastic wrap that doesn't tear properly

short people who request the exit row

133

getting caught listening to someone's conversation

eavesdroppers

dunking your earbud in your coffee and mildly electrocuting your other ear

hearing the songs you grew up with now played on the oldies station

being woken up to help move a dead passenger to the back row of your international flight

discovering your 38,000 frequent flyer miles have expired

seeing people water their lawns in the middle of the day in the middle of a drought

people who let their dogs shit on your lawn and leave it there

being told you should quit smoking for the billionth time

being made to feel guilty

vacuuming up the cord to your venetian blinds

discovering termites in your sofa

paying $3,500 to have your house tented for termites then discovering ants in your kitchen two days later

learning that ants like to eat dead termites

double dipping

prices that end in 99 cents

disconnect notices

overuse of the word "organic"

burning yourself on a hot seatbelt buckle

**being more appetizing to mosquitoes
than everyone else around you**

receiving the suggestion that you sit in the front of
the canoe because your girlfriend appears to be
stronger than you are

**throwing away the cassette tape collection you
lovingly created over two and a half decades**

seeing your bald spot for the first time

hearing your own voice on a recording

being told to stop feeling sorry for yourself

**pulling a muscle during the warm-up exercises of
your first karate class**

losing your balance in yoga class
and falling into the gong

**realizing you were conceived
by accident**

being kicked awake
by a fitful sleeper

**being elbowed in the face
by a fitful sleeper**

working for hundreds of hours
on a Web site that nobody
ends up going to

making a movie that gets compared to *Ishtar*

being told you're out of your league

quitting your job, then begging for it back

painting your entire apartment a bold red before
realizing it looks like the lair of a serial killer

paying a storage facility to hold junk you're
never going to need again

thinking you might take up smoking cigars, then
barfing into a planter 10 minutes later

buying a house with your boyfriend
and then breaking up

owing more on your mortgage than
your house is worth

holding out for a better price and eventually
selling for a huge loss

spilling water on your journal
and washing away the first 50 pages

saving a bottle of wine
for a special occasion
then discovering
it's turned to vinegar

being known as
so-and-so's sister

being "between jobs
at the moment"

discovering a pile of love
letters to your wife
from another man

admitting you haven't flossed
since your last dental exam

rude awakenings

walking out of the bathroom with your skirt
tucked into your panty hose

worrying that you might be "late"

waiting for someone who's always late

trying to please someone who's never satisfied

not getting along with your boyfriend's friends

being the only bad dancer at a Puerto Rican wedding

realizing you're about to break up

getting pulled over by a K-9 cop car for
having illegal tinting on your windows when
you happen to have pot in the glove compartment

locking your keys in the trunk of your rental car

driving a car with broken a/c and
windows that don't roll down

staring at a blank page

reading the same line in a book
over and over

wiping off someone else's pee
from the toilet seat

feeling like there might be a
spider in your hair

suspecting you're
about to get fired

getting stuck with a
Canadian quarter

managing to become an astronaut,
getting selected for a mission,
flying 250,000 miles to the moon,
and having to stay inside the lunar lander

**people who hang handicap signs in their cars
when they aren't handicapped**

leaving a big tip in the tip jar but timing it poorly
so you don't get visual credit for it and appear to
have stiffed the cute barista

**planning the perfect wedding in Mexico
that no one comes to because they're afraid
of getting swine flu**

being asked to repeat something several times that
was barely worth saying in the first place

**flipping someone off for driving like a moron before
realizing you've had your blinker on for five miles**

going deaf

going blind

going the wrong direction on a
highway exit ramp

getting roofied

losing on a technicality

losing your access privileges

people who refuse to believe
global warming is real

swirlies

SARS

the bends

arson

being out-of-order

having your favorite show
canceled

having no one to turn to

having no idea what you're doing

getting in over your head

being told to buck up

being told, "I told you so"

knowing you could have done something

having your funding cut

having to choose the lesser of two evils

taking the fall

facing the music

paying the piper

slowly going insane

spiraling out of control

getting screwed over

the banking industry

hecklers

bad delivery

bad crowds

bad audiences

being lied to

being the butt of a joke

being at the center of

a media circus

being publicly humiliated

batting someone in the

face with a softball

slicing off the tip of

your finger with an

industrial meat slicer

driving around for 45 minutes looking for parking

working a double

working a triple

forgetting your lunch

having your wig blown off

having your toupee carried off by a dog

toupees

having your used condom carried
into a dinner party by your cat

delivering bad news

having your project shelved

waiting to tell someone something great only
they die on the way to meet you

being told by Facebook you should reconnect
with someone who's dead

picking up your
blown-over garbage

waiting outside Home Depot
with 50 other guys
looking for work

bonuses for people who suck
at their jobs

worst-case scenarios

waiting in vain

being bumped from the schedule

being mauled by your pet tiger

putting your foot in your mouth

being sent off to boarding school

being stalked

pandering

floundering

missing a free throw

being ashamed of your body

being mistreated

negative energy

negative account balances

culling

shooting 6,000 thirsty camels during a drought

regrettable decisions

receding hairlines

receding gums

repressed feelings

rug burns

roid ragers

rashes

having a cap popped in your ass

being addicted

being paid to take a dive

having your order messed up

being bitch slapped

being blown off

falling off a ladder

falling off a roof

crabgrass

people who throw garbage out
their car windows

**dreams that remind you of
shit you're trying to forget**

complaining about your job in an e-mail and
inadvertently cc'ing your boss who then fires you

playing dreidel

fat-free milk in coffee

wishing things could be different

wasting away

crumbs in your keyboard

people who constantly forward you
joke e-mails that aren't funny

**people who constantly forward you e-mails
supporting their lame political agendas**

rancor

**reconnecting with people you
don't want to reconnect with**

going overbudget

**pretending your child has been
carried off by a weather balloon**

enablers

codependency

twisting your ankle

looking under your refrigerator

backing over a fire hydrant

**seeing what your skin looks like
under ultraviolet lighting**

waking up

being the new kid

trying to stop biting your nails

forgetting your charger

cavity searches

driving around on Christmas Eve in search of a
whole vanilla bean for a stupid recipe

movie ticket prices

popcorn prices

pocket calls

scratched records

hidden fees

UTIs

bringing home someone else's groceries

bad sequels

ghetto grocery stores

getting in over your head

commitment issues

static cling

sinkholes

sex scandals

broken water mains

freezer burn

trying to act inconspicuous in
the bookstore as you check out
a girl and then discover you're
perusing in the gay and lesbian
self-help section

stained couch cushions

cracked skin

crumbling under pressure

caving on your principles

clinging with desperation

the clap

carbon footprints

veiled threats

smelly vaginas

the blame game

the rat race

the death spiral

the way things are

landlords who don't fix things

tenants who don't take care of things

bad carpets

low ceilings

tiny ovens

tiny living rooms where there's no
good place to put a sofa

bad reception

bland food

blind spots

overbearing husbands

underperforming portfolios

torn book jackets

misfiled documents

missing persons

missed opportunities

misogynists

labor disputes

war profiteers

predatory lending practices

pockmarks

potted meat

bed spins

Bible-thumpers

PMS

teachers' salaries

clinical depression

suicide

famine

oil dependency

war

cancer

going in without an exit strategy

**calling someone's bluff then finding out
they weren't bluffing**

acting all smug and then being wrong

smug assholes

school bullies

bad dye jobs

death

taxes

typos

bad reviews

other people's books of lists

running out of space

feeling like the end is near

**running out of things to complain
about complainers**

being negative

having trouble finding closure

being left wanting more . . .

My deepest thanks to:

Wendy Weitz
Doris Schwartz
Jane Wagner
Joel Mendelson
Irene Shoiket
Brooke Kaplan
Ryan Kaplan
Erica Borenstein
Josh Brown
Sunil Nayar
Rose Gray
Norman Cohen
Chris Dingess
Marcello Picone

About the Author

Jason Kaplan is the author and illustrator of *Things that Suck*. He was raised in Potomac, Maryland, and studied English literature and anthropology at Washington University in St. Louis. He currently lives in Los Angeles.

that blows.

no, it sucks.